Anonymous

Essays on the Malt Liquor Question

Anonymous

Essays on the Malt Liquor Question

ISBN/EAN: 9783337330897

Printed in Europe, USA, Canada, Australia, Japan

Cover: Foto ©Thomas Meinert / pixelio.de

More available books at **www.hansebooks.com**

1876.

BREWERS' INDUSTRIAL EXHIBITION,

Centennial Grounds, Fairmount Park, Philadelphia.

MAIN EXHIBITION BUILDING.

THIS building is in the form of a parallelogram, extending east and west 1,880 feet in length, and north and south 464 feet in width.

The larger portion of the structure is one story in height, and shows the main cornice upon the outside at 45 feet above the ground, the interior height being 70 feet. At the centre of the longer sides are projections 416 feet in length, and in the centre of the shorter sides or ends of the building are projections 216 feet in length. In these projections, in the centre of the four sides, are located the main entrances, which are provided with arcades upon the ground floor, and central façades extending to the height of 90 feet.

The EAST ENTRANCE forms the principal approach for carriages, visitors being allowed to alight at the doors of the building under cover of the arcade.

The SOUTH ENTRANCE is the principal approach from street cars, the ticket offices being located upon the line of ELM AVENUE, with covered ways provided for entrance into the building itself.

The MAIN PORTAL on the north side communicates directly with the ART GALLERY, and the MAIN PORTAL on the west side gives the main passage way to the MACHINERY and AGRICULTURAL HALLS.

Upon the corners of the building there are four towers 75 feet in height, and between the towers and the central projections or entrances, there is a lower roof introduced showing a cornice at 24 feet above the ground.

In order to obtain a central feature for the building as a whole, the roof over the central part, for 184 feet square, has been raised above the surrounding portion, and four towers, 48 feet square, rising to 120 feet in height, have been introduced at the corners of the elevated roof.

The areas are covered as follows:

Ground Floor, - - - - - - - - - - - -	872,320 square feet.		20.02 acres.
Upper Floors in projections - - - - - -	37,344	" "	.85	"
" " in towers - - - - - - - - -	26,344	" "	.60	"
	936,008		21.47	

ART GALLERY.

This structure, which is one of the affixes to the great Exhibition, is located on a line parallel with and northward of the Main Exhibition Building. It is on the most commanding portion of the great LANSDOWNE PLATEAU, and looks southward over the city. It is elevated on a terrace 6 feet above the general level of this plateau, which itself is an eminence 116 feet above the level of the Schuylkill River. The style of the entire structure is modern renaissance. The materials are granite, glass, and iron. No wood is used in the construction, and the building is thoroughly fireproof. The structure is 365 feet in length, 210 feet in width, and 59 feet in height, over a spacious basement 12 feet in height, and is surmounted by a dome.

MAY 10TH — NOVEMBER 10TH 1876.

PHILADELPHIA U. S. AMERICA

INTERNATIONAL EXHIBITION.

1876

1776

MAIN EXHIBITION BUILDING.

DETAILS.

EXTERIOR—1. THE MAIN FRONT.—The main front looks southward; it displays three distinctive features:—*First.* A main entrance in the centre of the structure, consisting of three colossal arched door-ways of equal dimensions. *Second.* A pavilion at each end. *Third.* Two arcades connecting the pavilions with the centre; central section, 95 feet long, 72 feet high; pavilions, 45 feet long, 60 feet high; arcades, each, 90 feet long, 40 feet high.

The front or south face of the central section displays a rise of thirteen steps to the entrance, 70 feet wide. The entrance is by three arched door-ways, each 40 feet high and 15 feet wide, opening into a hall. Between the arches of the door-ways are clusters of columns terminating in emblematic designs illustrative of science and art.

The doors, which are of iron, are relieved by bronze panels, having the coats of arms of all the States and Territories. In the centre of the main frieze is the United States coat of arms. The main cornice is surmounted by a balustrade with candelabras. At either end is an allegorical figure representing science and art.

The dome rises from the centre of the structure to the height of 150 feet from the ground. It is of glass and iron, and of a unique design; it terminates in a colossal bell—from which the figure of Columbia rises with protecting hands. A figure of colossal size stands at each corner of the base of the dome. These figures typify the four quarters of the globe.

Each pavilion displays a window 30 feet high and 12 feet wide; it is also ornamented with tile-work, wreaths of oak and laurel, thirteen stars in the frieze, and a colossal eagle at each of its four corners. The arcades, a general feature in the old Roman villas, but entirely novel here, are intended to screen the long walls of the gallery. These each consist of five groined arches; these arcades form promenades looking outward over the grounds and inward over open gardens, which extend back to the main wall of the building. These garden plats are each 90 feet long and 36 feet deep, ornamented in the centre with fountains and designed for the display of statuary. A stair-way from the gardens reaches the upper line of these arcades, forming a second promenade 35 feet above the ground. Its balustrade is ornamented with vases, and is designed ultimately for statues. The cornices, the atticas, and the crestings throughout are highly ornamented. The walls of the east and west sides of the structure display the pavilions and the walls of the picture galleries, and are relieved by five niches designed for statues; the frieze is richly ornamented—above it the central dome shows to great advantage.

The rear or north front is of the same general character as the main front, but in place of the arcade is a series of arched windows, twelve in number, with an entrance in the centre; in all, thirteen openings above, in an unbroken line, extending the entire length of the structure; between the pavilions is the grand balcony—a promenade 275 feet long and 45 feet wide, and elevated 40 feet above the ground, overlooking northward the whole panorama of the park grounds. The main entrance opens on a hall 82 feet long, 60 feet wide, and 53 feet high, decorated in the modern renaissance style; on the farther side of this hall, three door-ways, each 16 feet wide and 25 feet high, open into the centre hall; this hall is 83 feet square, the ceiling of the dome rising over it 80 feet in height. From its east and west sides extend the galleries, each 98 feet long, 84 feet wide, and 35 feet in height. The centre hall and galleries form one grand hall 287 feet long and 85 feet wide. From the two galleries, doorways open into two smaller galleries, 28 feet wide and 89 feet long. These open north and south into private apartments, which connect with the pavilion rooms,

PHILADELPHIA U. S. AMERICA

MAY 10TH ○ NOVEMBER 10TH 1876.

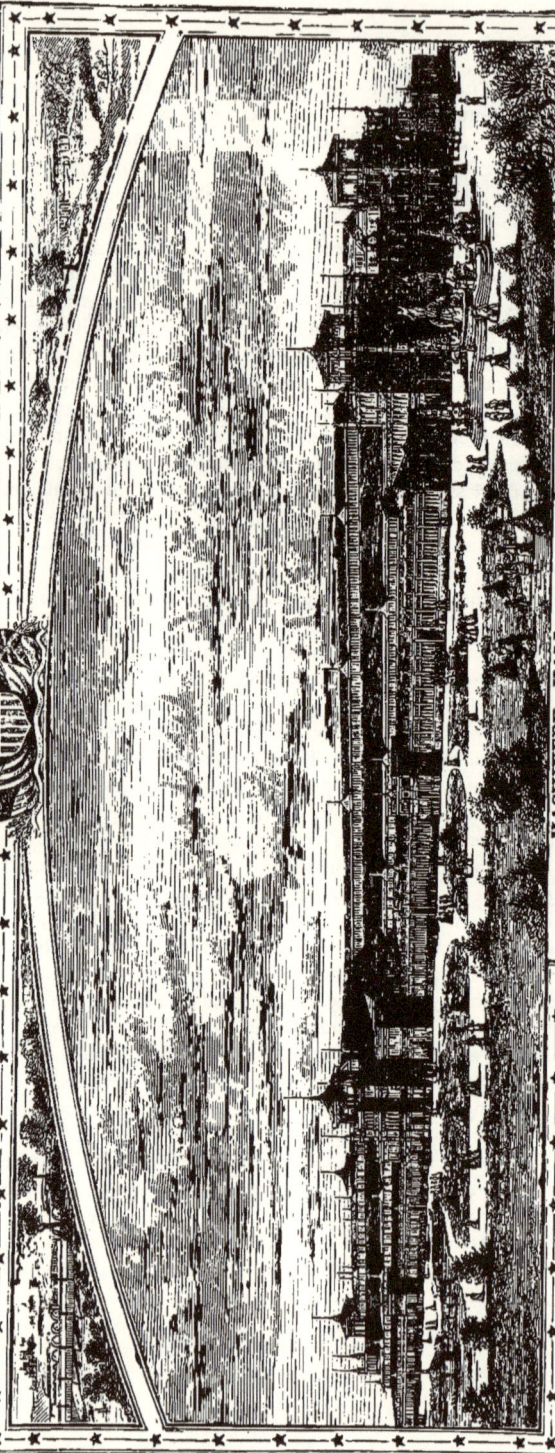

INTERNATIONAL EXHIBITION.

1776

1876

MACHINERY HALL

forming two side galleries 210 feet long Along the whole length of the north side of the main galleries and central hall extends a corridor 14 feet wide, which opens on its northerly line into a series of private rooms, thirteen in number, designed for studios and smaller exhibition rooms. All the galleries and the central hall are lighted from above; the pavilions and studios are lighted from the sides. The pavilions and central hall are designed especially for exhibitions of sculpture.

MACHINERY BUILDING.

This structure is located west of the intersection of Belmont and Elm Avenues, at a distance of 542 feet from the west front of the Main Exhibition Building, and 274 feet from the north side of Elm Avenue. The north front of the Building will be upon the same line as that of the Main Exhibition Building, thus presenting a frontage of 3,824 feet from the east to the west ends of the Exhibition Buildings upon the principal avenue within the grounds.

The building consists of the Main Hall, 360 feet wide by 1,402 feet long, and an annex on the south side of 208 feet by 210 feet. The entire area covered by the Main Hall and annex is 558,440 square feet, or 12.82 acres. Including the upper floors the building provides 14 acres of floor space.

The principal portion of the structure is one story in height, showing the main cornice upon the outside at 40 feet from the ground, the interior height to the top of the ventilators in the avenues being 70 feet, and in the aisles 40 feet. To break the long lines upon the exterior, projections have been introduced upon the four sides, and the main entrances finished with façades, extending to 78 feet in height. The east entrance forms the principal approach from street-cars, from the Main Exhibition Building, and from the railroad depot. Along the south side are placed the boiler-houses and such other buildings for special kinds of machinery as may be required. The west entrance affords the most direct communication with George's Hill, which point affords the best view of the entire Exhibition grounds.

The building admits of the most complete system of shafting, the facilities in this respect being very superior. Eight main lines being introduced, extending almost the entire length of the structure, and counter-shafts introduced into the aisles at any point. The hangers are attached either to the wooden horizontal ties of the 60-feet span roof trusses, or to brackets especially designed for the purpose, projecting from the columns, in either case at the height of 20 feet from the floor.

The annex for hydraulic machines contains a tank 60 feet by 160 feet, with 10 feet depth of water. In connection with this is hydraulic machinery exhibited in full operation. At the south end of this tank is a water-fall 35 feet high by 40 feet wide, supplied from the tank by the pumps on exhibition.

HORTICULTURAL BUILDING.

The liberal appropriations of the City of Philadelphia have provided the Horticultural Department of the Exhibition with an extremely ornate and commodious building, which is to remain in permanence as an ornament of Fairmount Park. It is located on the Lansdowne Terrace, a short distance north of the Main Building and Art Gallery, and has a commanding view of the Schuylkill River and the northwestern portion of the city. The design is in the Mauresque style of architecture of the twelfth century, the principal materials externally being iron and glass. The

PHILADELPHIA U. S. AMERICA

MAY 10TH - NOVEMBER 10TH 1876.

INTERNATIONAL EXHIBITION.

HORTICULTURAL HALL.

1776

1876

length of the building is 383 feet; width, 193 feet, and height to the top of the lantern, 72 feet.

The main floor is occupied by the central conservatory, 230 by 80 feet, and 55 feet high, surmounted by a lantern 170 feet long, 20 feet wide, and 14 feet high. Running entirely around this conservatory, at a height of 20 feet from the floor, is a gallery 5 feet wide. On the north and south sides of this principal room are four forcing-houses for the propagation of young plants, each of them 100 by 30 feet, covered with curved roofs of iron and glass. Dividing the two forcing-houses in each of these sides is a vestibule 30 feet square. At the centre of the east and west ends are similar vestibules, on either side of which are the restaurants, reception-room, offices, &c. From the vestibules ornamental stair-ways lead to the internal galleries of the conservatory, as well as to the four external galleries, each 100 feet long and 10 feet wide, which surmount the roofs of the forcing-houses. These external galleries are connected with a grand promenade, formed by the roofs of the rooms on the ground floor, which has a superficial area of 1,800 square yards.

The east and west entrances are approached by flights of blue-marble steps from terraces 80 by 20 feet, in the centre of each of which stands an open kiosque 20 feet in diameter. The angles of the main conservatory are adorned with eight ornamental fountains. The corridors which connect the conservatory with the surrounding rooms open fine vistas in every direction.

In the basement, which is of fire-proof construction, are the kitchen, store-rooms, coal-houses, ash-pits, heating arrangements, etc.

AGRICULTURAL BUILDING.

This structure stands north of the Horticultural Building, and on the eastern side of Belmont Avenue. It illustrates a novel combination of materials, and was erected within a few months. Its materials are wood and glass. It consists of a long nave crossed by three transepts, both nave and transept being composed of Howe truss arches of a Gothic form. The nave is 820 feet in length by 125 feet in width, with a height of 75 feet from the floor to the point of the arch. The central transept is of the same height, and a breadth of 100 feet, the two end transepts 70 feet high and 80 feet wide.

The four courts enclosed between the nave and transepts, and also the four spaces at the corners of the building, having the nave and end transepts for two of their sides, are roofed and form valuable spaces for exhibits. Thus the ground plan of the building forms a parallelogram of 540 by 820 feet, covering a space of above ten acres. In its immediate vicinity are the stock-yards for the exhibition of horses, cattle, sheep, swine, poultry, etc.

This comprehensive system of building, viz.:

MAIN BUILDING,	-	-	-	-	covering 21.47 acres.
ART GALLERY,	-	-	-	-	covering 1.05 acres.
MACHINERY BUILDING,				-	covering 14.00 acres.
HORTICULTURAL BUILDING,			-	-	covering 1.05 acres.
AGRICULTURAL BUILDING,	-		-	-	covering 10.15 acres.

provides for the accommodation of the seven departments of the classification.

There are, in addition to these buildings, a number of smaller structures for the administration of the Exhibition.

MAY 10TH ∘ NOVEMBER 10TH 1876.

PHILADELPHIA U. S. AMERICA

INTERNATIONAL EXHIBITION.

AGRICULTURAL HALL.

1876

1776

Besides the Exhibition buildings proper, numerous applications have been made by manufacturers, and by the commissions of foreign governments for permission to erect pavilions and various ornamental and useful structures within the Exhibition grounds. A number of fountains, memorial statues and other decorative objects are in preparation, under the auspices of local organizations. Not the least among which is the Brewers' Building.

BREWERS' BUILDING.

This building compares very favorably with any structure on the Centennial grounds erected by private enterprise, and is a credit to the trade it represents. The dimensions are 272 feet long, by 96 feet wide. The centre tower has an elevation of 60 feet, and the wings 28 feet. It was designed by H. J. Schwarzmann, the architect of the Memorial Hall and the Horticultural Hall, and erected by J. B. Doyle. The contents of Building form a complete Brewers' Industrial Exhibition of Malt Liquor, Malt, Hops and all the mechanical appliances used in each branch of the Brewing business. In addition to the Main Hall a building has also been provided for the storage of malt liquor for exhibition and competition, 70 feet by 80 feet, double walls filled in, divided into three compartments: one compartment, 25 by 80 feet, for the storage of ale in bulk; another compartment, the same dimensions, for malt liquor on draught, and the centre compartment, 20 by 80 feet, over which is an ice-box, to hold four feet in depth of ice, for the storage of lager-beer. The uniform temperature of the middle compartment is 45° Fahr., and of the two side compartments, 56° Fahr. There are samples of malt liquors constantly on draught, and visitors are invited, with the permission of the Directors, to discuss the merits of the same.

PHILADELPHIA U. S. AMERICA

MAY 10TH ~ NOVEMBER 10TH 1876.

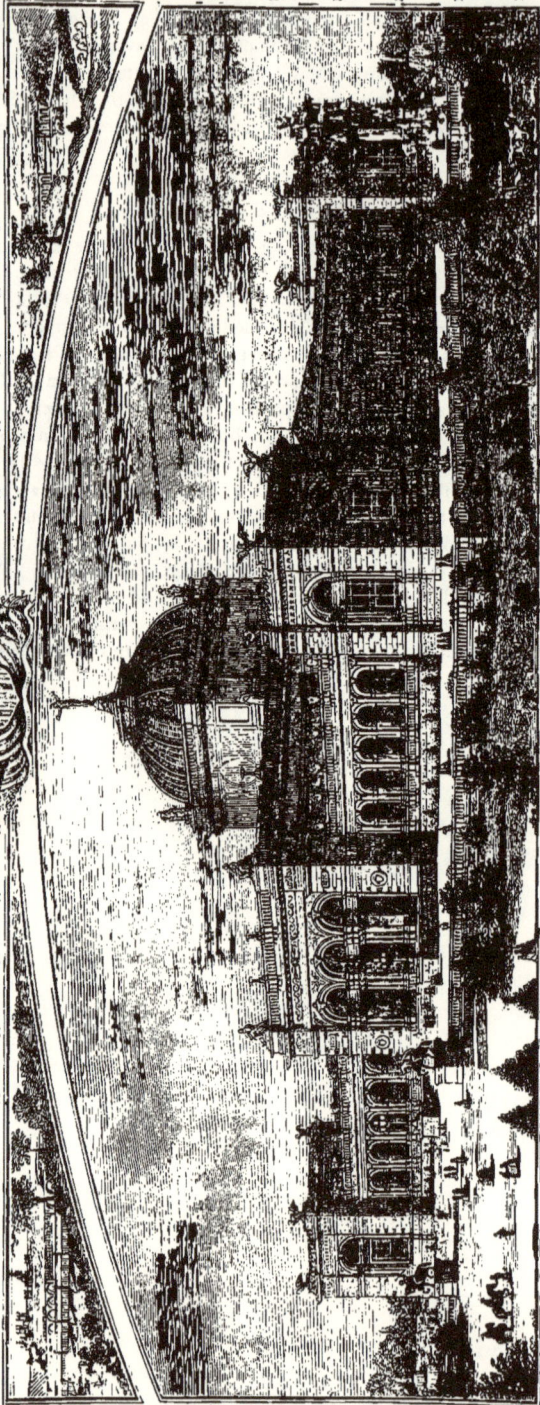

INTERNATIONAL EXHIBITION.

1776

1876

ART GALLERY.

MALT LIQUORS.

In this Centennial year of our Republic, when, here in this city, where our independence was first proclaimed, we have displayed before us, in magnificent array, the products of art, science and industry from every part of the habitable globe, there to challenge comparison with similar products of our own, to enlighten us on the progress of the world at large, to teach us the true story of our own advancement, and to be an incentive to us at the outset of our second century's march of civilization, it would be strange, on the part of any branch of industry, and a dereliction of duty, should it neglect, by every legitimate means, to place itself in the best possible light before the world. Above all others, this becomes necessary for the industry represented by brewers, because, either from ignorance or prejudice, it has many enemies to its progress unknown to other branches of trade, and further, because it is willfully or ignorantly classed with productions inimical to the welfare of society.

That a brewer is just as necessary to the commonweal as a butcher, a baker, a tailor, a builder, or any other economic industry, is proven by the present position of the trade in the United States. There are, according to the latest returns, at present in active operation 2,600 breweries, producing annually for sale and consumption, in round figures, two hundred and eighty-five millions (285,000,000) of gallons of malt liquors, besides numerous private breweries where malt liquor is not made for sale, and which do not come under the Internal Revenue regulations, and consequently are not enumerated. By far the majority of these breweries have been erected during the last quarter of a century; not one of the present structures witnessed the first year of our independence, 1776, and but one or two the first year of this nineteenth century. The largest quantity of malt liquors produced in a year by a single brewery is four millions two hundred and twenty-five thousand (4,225,000) gallons. Of the trades more or less dependent upon brewers, scarcely an idea can be formed by the general public. From the agriculturist the brewer obtains barley for malt, other cereals for fodder, and hops. Respecting the culture of barley, the Commissioner of Agriculture in Washington reports as follows: "There were in 1874, 1,580,626 acres under cultivation with barley, which produced 32,552,500 bushels, at a value of $29,983,769. The average yield per acre was 20.6 bushels; the average price per bushel was 92.1 cents, and the average value of barley produced per acre, $18.96, against $13.40 with Indian corn, $11.66 with wheat, $11.52 with rye, $11.47 with oats,—barley yielding next to potatoes and tobacco the highest value per acre. According to the money value, the annual produce of barley is only second to Indian corn, hay, wheat, cotton, oats and potatoes; being, therefore, the seventh agricultural staple article of the country, and nearly seven millions of dollars higher in value than that of tobacco." Of hops, the last Agricultural census reports a total production in the United States of twenty-five million four hundred and fifty-six thousand six hundred and sixty-nine (25,456,669) pounds. The arborculturist supplies the brewer with oak, cedar, and pine for barrels, vats, and tuns, and other timber for building purposes. Commerce furnishes grain dealers and importers, because our own country does not yet supply all the necessities of the trade.

Next comes the maltster, a business so unostentatious and unobtrusive, and so little understood that cities have been known to possess extensive malt-houses, which for years have been looked upon by the general public as commercial warehouses or bonded stores, and yet these malt-houses number nearly four hundred (400); of real estate value, ten million three hundred and sixty-five thousand five hundred (10,-365,500) dollars; having malting capacity of nineteen million one hundred and fifty-seven thousand one hundred (19,157,100) bushels; in the production of which is engaged capital amounting to thirteen million seven hundred and eight thousand (13,708,000) dollars; two thousand five hundred (2,500) men are employed, whose annual wages amount to one million eighty-six thousand nine hundred (1,086,900) dollars. In addition to this enormous trade the Commissioner of Agriculture reports that six million two hundred and fifty-four thousand seven hundred and seventy-three (6,254,773) bushels were imported from Canada and other foreign countries. There are, in addition to these, a large number of brewers who malt especially for their own use, who are not included in these figures.

In order that the extent of the brewing, malting, and hop trades may be fully understood, we present the following figures, based upon the most reliable data :—

CAPITAL.

Capital invested in breweries (estimated at \$10 upon every barrel of malt liquor produced), - - - -	\$88,806,290
Capital invested in malt-houses, - - - - -	24,094,500
Value of land under cultivation for barley, - - -	63,225,040
Value of land under cultivation for hops, - - - -	2,360,520

LABOR.

There are employed in breweries (estimating one man for every 800 barrels of malt liquor produced), - - -	men, 11,100	Annual wages,	\$5,772,000
There are employed in malt-houses (for the season), 7 months,	men, 2,500	"	wages,	1,086,500
In the culture of barley (one man to every 100 acres),	men, 15,806	"	wages,	4,742,000
In the culture of hops (one man to every 10 acres), - -	men, 5,901	"	wages,	1,770,300

LAND

Under cultivation for barley, - - - - - acres,	1,580,626
Under cultivation for hops, - -, - - - acres,	59,013
Under cultivation for other cereals (fodder, etc.), - - -	

After these come the long array of professional men, as architects, civil engineers; of artificers and tradesmen, as masons, builders, carpenters, coopers, machinists, wagon-makers, laborers, etc., etc., so numerous that only by a collective exhibition of their productions can an approximate idea of their extent be conceived.

Such, then, is the brewing trade in the United States, in this centennial year, and it is not the least part of the argument in favor of this industry that it does so exist; yet its very extent and prosperity appear to excite the opposition of the unwise. Under these circumstances, it becomes necessary to consider the use and abuse of malt liquors, from the three points most liable to attack.

In discussing the economic view of the question we take the fifth definition of Webster "relating to the means of living, or the resources and wealth of a community." As we before stated, the trade, business or calling of a brewer is just so much an integral part of a State as any other necessary calling, and without it something would be lacking for the general good. In striking illustration of this, we will compare it with another industry, that of the baker. The process of making bread, according to *Dr. Ure*, is as follows: When a baker intends to make a batch of bread, his first care is, in technical language, to stir a ferment by means of yeast, water, flour and potatoes. This is allowed to operate for some hours, and then thickened with flour; more water being added, which constitutes what is called the "sponge," which is kept in a warm situation when the fermentation begins. The result of this fermentation is carbonic acid, induced, under the influence of water, by the action of the gluten upon the starch, a portion of which is converted thereby into sugar, and then into alcohol. It is then baked. Thus, a well-baked loaf is composed of an infinite number of cellules, filled with carbonic acid gas, and apparently lined with a glutinous membrane of a silky softness. It is this which gives the light, elastic, porous constitution to bread. It is true bread may be made by an artificial fermentation, but, in this respect, Liebig remarks—speaking of the fermentation obtained by yeast—"Yeast fermentation is not only the best and simplest, but likewise the most economical way of imparting porosity to bread." Thus showing, in a remarkable manner, the affinity existing between bread and beer. The proportion of water in bread is 42, and of flour 58.

The production of malt liquor bears a striking similarity to the manufacture of bread, the chief difference being in the quantity of grain employed, and the amount of water added. The one, intended to produce a solid food, is baked; the other, to produce a liquid refreshment, is boiled. The process of making beer is as follows : A certain quantity of malted barley is taken and ground; it is then mashed with hot water, the sweet liquor or wort extracted, a proportion of hops added; the whole is then boiled until the preservative quality as well as the aroma of the hop is obtained. It is then allowed to cool, and afterward fermented with yeast to produce the small quantity of alcohol it contains, and to give it life. According to *Otto*, lager-beer contains 91.0 water, 5.4 malt extract, 3.50 alcohol, and the remainder, making in all 100 parts, carbonic acid, etc. Ale and porter differ only in a slight additional percentage of alcohol and a larger amount of solid extract. In the ordinary process of bread fermentation, a portion of the sugar contained in the flour is decomposed and converted into alcohol. It has been heretofore supposed that by the heat of baking, the whole of this alcohol was expelled, but recent experiments indicate that a perceptible amount of alcohol still remains in yeast-raised bread after baking. The result of six experiments showed that one-third of one per cent. in weight of alcohol was obtainable from fresh baked bread; but the quantity of alcohol was much less in stale bread. From forty loaves of fresh bread, two pounds each, alcohol equal to one bottle of port wine may be extracted.

Such, then, is the process, comparatively, of the manufacture of beer and of bread, both equally necessary to our well-being, for if it were a calamity to be deprived of one, so would it be of the other. Malt liquors have conferred benefits upon mankind which cannot be overestimated; containing, as they do, a large proportion of water from which all organic impurities are eliminated, a certain quantity of nutritive malt extract, a small percentage of pure alcohol—obtained by fermentation, and entirely free from the injurious properties it acquires in distillation,—together with some of the carbonic acid gas, so thoroughly approved of by consumers of sodas. It offers to the public a beverage at once healthy, nutritious, and mildly stimulating, and as refreshing and exhilarating as tea, coffee or cocoa." Those who travel know very well the injurious effects of change of water upon the human system; in no two districts are the waters alike, and we could point to many instances where a change from East to West, or from North to South, and the consequent change of water, has resulted in positively disastrous effects upon individuals. The brewers of malt liquors, in cities along the course of our great rivers, know well how their efforts tend to the public welfare. Therefore the establishment of a brewery is commendable; for everywhere exists in nature something that may be improved by art, and one of the chief distinctions between civilized communities and savage life is that the one knows best how to make this improvement, and in the use of alcoholic beverages this distinction is most apparent.

The superiority of malt liquors, as a wholesome and refreshing beverage, has perhaps never before been so severely tested as in the late war between Germany and France; and it may with truth be asserted that it has triumphantly withstood the trial, and fully maintained its reputation. In their official report to the Medical Board the German military surgeons bear witness to the advantage of beer over wine, especially the poor common wines of the Champagne, and the other wine-producing parts of the country they took possession of, and still to a certain extent occupy. They state it to be the peculiarly refreshing property of the carbonic acid gas contained in beer that makes it such a grateful beverage, not only to the healthy, after a long and fatiguing march, or when fairly worn out by the excitement of a day's hard fighting. But they lay much greater stress on the use of beer in the hospitals and field ambulances, and administered it when it could be obtained, with great success, as a cordial, both to the wounded and convalescent soldiers placed for the time under their medical care. They add the interesting fact, founded on their experience gathered in the late campaign, that the wounded invariably evince a great longing for beer, and that their very first request, when brought into the hospital for medical treatment, with shattered limbs, or after undergoing a severe and painful operation, is for a glass of beer to slake their thirst, and compose and fortify their unstrung nerves. This natural impulse of longing for beer, as a restorative, was nowhere more conspicuous than among the soldiers on exposed outpost duty during the cold wintry weather at the time of the blockade and siege of Paris, where, on account of the scarcity of the article, the common soldiers did not hesitate to pay the followers of the army as much as ninepence and a shilling for a very small glass, containing only a few mouthfuls of beer. The report of the Director-General of the Army Medical Staff concludes with a strong recommendation, not only to supply the soldiers with rations of beer, instead of spirits, when employed on active duty in time of war, but also to introduce it as the general beverage for the army in time of peace, and when on home service.

The noblest philosophy of life, since extremes must, perforce, exist, is compromise. Temperance, then, is the truest medium between total abstinence and excess; and malt liquors, above all, are the medium between ardent spirits and water.

Professor Moleschott, in his Chemistry of Food, thus speaks of beer: "The weak alcoholic solution of beer contains nearly the same proportion of albumen as found in fruits, some sugar and gum; and in addition to these, a peculiar constituent of the hops, soluble in water, consisting of carbon, hydrogen and oxygen, which from its bitter taste is called the bitter principle of the hop." He then proceeds: "Fermented liquors, taken in moderation, increase the secretion of the digestive juices, and promote the solution of the food;" and further, "A good beer partakes of all the advantage of the alcoholic beverages, and, at the same time, usefully quenches the thirst by its more abundant amount of water. Hence this beverage is particularly adapted to satisfy the frequent thirst caused by bodily exertion ; it is, therefore, a laudable custom to refresh artisans, who have to work hard, in the morning and afternoon with a glass of ale ; this beverage, by its proportionate amount of albumen, which is equal to that of fruit, supplies even a direct substitute for food." Richmond Sheen adds testimony to the following effect :—" That beer is nutritive and, when used in moderation, salubrious, can scarcely be doubted. It proves a refreshing drink, and an agreeable and valuable stimulus and support to those who have to undergo much bodily fatigue. The laborer, who has repeatedly experienced its invigorating property, will by no means admit the truth of the assertion, that a half-pound loaf and a pint of water yield more nourishment than a pint of beer." Robert Ward, in his fallacies of teetotalism, thus remarks : " I have said that alcoholic liquors may be something better than either food or physic. We do not always want food, we rarely require physic. A glass of wine or beer may be useful refreshment when the stomach is not prepared for the reception of the one, and the system has no need of the other. Excessive physical labor, long endurance of hunger, or anything which has a debilitating influence, more or less affects the appetite for solid food, and unfits the stomach for its reception. At such times alcoholic liquors are found to have a beneficial effect upon some constitutions, both in affording present refreshment, and in preparing the system for more substantial diet, &c., &c. At a time of mental depression we take a glass of wine or beer, for the same reason that at a time of physical depression we take our dinner—because appetite invites us to the entertainment, and the sense of taste approves of the refreshment." Dr. T. K. Chambers says: "It is certain that the habitual daily use of a small allowance of alcoholic drink bestows on a large class the nervous energy necessary to digest food enough to exist upon, and to get through other vital functions. By this stimulus they are enabled to be useful members of society, instead of the mere drones they must become during the rest of their existence, under a total abstinence regimen."

This brings us to the Social Aspect of the Malt Liquor Question. It has been urged that the production and sale of malt liquor is subversive of public morals; such is not the case, for experience demonstrates precisely the opposite. Dr. Scoffern, of the School of Chemistry, London, speaks thus definitely and distinctly : "I believe alcoholic drinks, taken within limits of temperance, to be a good and rational means of developing the mental and bodily powers of man. I cannot join in the gratulations of those who now so enthusiastically enjoy the blessings, as they say, of total abstinence. I have seen something of the operation of this enthusiasm, not only in England and Ireland, but in the native city of the originator of the movement; and even taking the low ground of argument, that a pledged abstainer *is* a drunkard saved, I find it impossible to accede to that proposition in all its universality. According to my experience, a pledged abstainer is too frequently a man who drinks in secret, thus adding hypocrisy to the other sin." It is therefore most unwise to interfere with the social habits of a people, and it is dangerous for a State to do so.

Here is some evidence rendered before a State Committee inquiring into the action of restrictive laws. The Hon. James H. Duncan, of Haverhill, says: "My observations and convictions are, that temperance has not been promoted by the prohibitory law; that the temperance of our people is not so good now as before the passage of the law; it has had no efficacy in checking intemperance and the evils that result from it;

2

it has been productive of more mischief than good, and I think it an unwise act. It is impossible to make that a crime which is not made a crime by the divine law, and the use of beer, wine or cider cannot by any effort be made a crime *per se;* yet the prohibitory statute makes it a crime to sell either, and worse, it is a crime for a carrier to carry them. No wonder that such a law demoralizes the community, for a vast amount of lying and fraud have been called into existence through its agency."

The Rev. George Putnam, D. D., says: " I believe and know that prohibitory law produces demoralization and disrespect for a law that cannot be enforced. It demoralizes jurors and witnesses. It demoralizes the buyers and sellers of liquors, inducing them to resort to all manner of frauds, tricks and evasions to do that unlawfully which they cannot do lawfully. It is injurious to the consciences of the people to be always violating this law; and, so far as liquor-drinking is concerned, the law has done no good."

Public testimony that such laws are a blunder, or worse, has been given by such men as John Quincy Adams; Professor Agassiz, of Cambridge; Rev. L. Bacon, D. D., of Connecticut: Professor Bigelow, of Boston; Professor Bowen, of Cambridge; General Burrell, of Roxbury; Professor Edward Clark, of Boston; ex-Governor Clifford; the Right Rev. M. Eastburn, D. D., of Boston; the late Governor Andrews; Oliver Wendell Holmes, of Boston; Hon. Joel Parker, of Cambridge; Hon. Judge Patch, of Lowell; ex-Governor Washburne, of Massachusetts; and numerous others.

The most remarkable phase of the time in which we live is the drawing of strong lines of demarcation between class and class. These lines once settled will require another epoch to remove them; and if any class deliberately choose, whether tacitly or actively, the wrong side of the line, there they will stay. It behooves us, then, to choose the right side; and that we believe to be the temperance side, where those who are besotted, whether with wine or self-conceit, will find no place. The social and political aspects of this malt liquor question go hand in hand. That it is considered neither just nor politic for the State to interfere with the habits and enjoyments of the people, as regards the consumption of alcoholic beverages, we may refer to the countries of Europe. In Germany, the State uses every possible means to provide for the people good wholesome malt liquor, which is the habitual beverage of the people, used by them at their meals and at their places of amusement, rendering them temperate, industrious, healthy, and contented; a people whose bravery is beyond question, and to whose peaceable, yet progressive qualities, our continent can bear good witness. Sweden recognizes the necessity of providing an alcoholic stimulant for the people, and for more than one hundred and fifty years its Government has devoted its attention and resources to provide the same, during which time that country has progressed considerably more than for five hundred years previously. In France, during the reign of Napoleon III., that monarch, finding the effects of the liquors used by the people, compounded of drugs, essences, and some alcohol, were seriously undermining and deteriorating the character of the French people, made overtures to some of the large brewers of England to establish breweries, in order to furnish the nation with good, wholesome malt liquors. Even at this very time, some of the leading *savants* of France, recognizing the source of the greatness of the country, and the indomitable courage of the people who were victorious in the late war, are now engaged in bringing science to bear on the subject of brewing, that they may be able to strike a blow at their former enemies in this direction, and develop in the people of France some of those virtues they have recognized in the Germans.

In England, the constant habit of the people is, as in Germany, to drink malt liquors, and the Government has never attempted to abolish the privilege. It is true there are licence laws to regulate the sale, but it has been proven that the more stringent those laws are, and they have been very often changed, the more ineffectual they become to prevent the evils they are intended to prevent.

The editor of the Chicago *Tribune*, writing from Germany, says: " Drunkenness is so rare and infrequent that it may be said not to exist. I have traveled thousands of miles through Germany in various directions, visiting nearly all the chief cities, and have made diligent inquiry of American Consuls and other well-informed persons, and received but one answer everywhere, viz.: ' No drunkenness among the Germans; public sentiment would not tolerate it; the habits of the country are all against it.' The reason of this freedom from inebriation is the total absence of whiskey, and the substitution of the milder beer. Whiskey is the ' hog ' that possesses the spirit of the raging devil, and the cultivation of whose intimate acquaintance makes so many beasts and loafers of Irishmen and Americans in the United States." Yet, at one time, Germany contained as drunken a people as could be found in Europe. Was this change in their habits caused by prohibitory liquor laws ? Not by any means. There were wise men at the head of the Government. They knew that the people would drink some stimulant. They cast about for the least injurious, and found the desired drink to be beer. From that time forth the Government nurtured the growth of hops and the manufacture of beer. The result is that there is no country in the world where there is less drunkenness than in Germany. Cannot our temperance folks take a lesson from Germany ?

So much for the social aspect of the malt liquor question. Politically, the question assumes a much more serious aspect, because, under the guise of public good, the meanest tyrannies are practiced, and it is claimed by those who oppose the production and sale of malt liquors, that, as citizens, they possess the right to legislate whenever what they consider their social rights are invaded by the social acts of another, and they claim that the sale and use of malt liquors invade those social rights; that it injures the right of security by stimulating disorder; that it destroys the right of equality by promoting poverty, and consequent taxation ; that it impedes the right to free and intellectual development, by weakening and demoralizing society. John Stuart Mill thus remarks on this social right question: " The theory of social rights, the like of which probably never before found its way into distinct language, being nothing short of this, that it is the absolute social right of every individual that every other individual shall act, in every respect, exactly as he ought; that whatsoever fails thereof, in the smallest particular, violates my social right, and entitles me to demand from the Legislature the removal of the grievance. So monstrous a principle is far more dangerous than any single interference with liberty; there is no violation of liberty which it could not justify ; it acknowledges no right to any freedom whatever, except, perhaps, to that of holding opinions in secret, without ever disclosing them. There are, in our day, gross usurpations upon the liberty of private life actually practiced, and still greater ones threatened, with some expectations of success; and opinions proposed which assert an unlimited right in the public not only to prohibit by law everything which it thinks wrong, but in order to get at what it thinks wrong, to prohibit any number of things which it admits to be innocent."

In pursuance of this doctrine there has occurred, experimentally only we trust, instances of tyranny unparalleled in history. So much so that in arguing a case of supposed damage against a liquor dealer, an eminent jurist makes the following remarks :

"When he who resides in a foreign land is contemplating removal to a new home, he takes up the Constitution of the United States, and of the several States, and reads them carefully. He there finds that no citizen or subject of any nation in the world receives such full, liberal and ample protection as does the citizen of the United States. He comes, but alas! he finds many of our State statutes are as tyrannical as our Constitution is liberal. Did foreigners understand our statute laws as well as they do the fundamental laws of the land, the tide of emigration would, no doubt, be turned in another direction."

The logical sequence of the evidence we have reviewed in this essay on the malt liquor question are the following conclusions, which are recommended to the consideration of the public:—

I. Malt liquors, from the small amount of alcohol they contain, combined with the nutritive extract of malt, the tonic properties of the hop, and the enlivening and refreshing properties of carbonic acid gas generated therein, are grateful to the appetite, pleasant to the taste, and beneficial to the human constitution; therefore, the appetite for them is perfectly natural, and ought to be temperately indulged, because the forcible interference with the proper gratification of any legitimate appetite is detrimental to a people, and dangerous to a country.

II. Where malt liquors are a national beverage, their use has not been found inimical to the welfare of society, and is perfectly consistent with habits of sobriety and temperance; therefore their production and sale ought, in every way, to be encouraged, for, when protected by enlightened laws, they add to the comfort and enjoyment of communities, and tend to diminish the consumption of that class of narcotics, compounds and stimulants, known to be positively injurious.

III. It is unwise and impolitic for the State to interfere with the domestic habits and enjoyment of a people on any pretense, more especially upon the pretense that the excesses of the few justify the interference with the liberty of the many, or that any paternal right or authority exists in a government over the people.

IN THE following we present to the reader an expression of opinion on the medical aspect of the malt liquor question, coming from competent medical authority. The writer is of assured medical, scientific and literary position, is actively engaged in the practice of his profession and well versed in its literature. If we do not wholly agree with the author's views upon some minor technical or collateral matters, still we print the essay exactly as written, believing that the position taken cannot be successfully assailed upon the medical and moral points involved.

THE MALT LIQUOR QUESTION IN ITS MEDICAL ASPECT.

THE *National Temperance Almanac* for 1876 estimates the value of the distilled spirits and fermented liquors consumed in the United States during the previous year, with the pecuniary loss and damage occasioned thereby, at a sum approaching fifteen hundred millions of dollars; and it sets down the number of drunkards in the country at six hundred thousand. It is so unusual to see a drunkard under twenty-five years, and so few of that class live over sixty, that we must draw this army of topers from between these ages. We may safely say that the proportion of male to female drunkards is as nineteen to one. If the figures given be correct, we find that forty years of the total abstinence agitation, with its open societies, secret orders, speeches, tracts, newspapers and prohibitory laws, assisted by the outcry of the ignorant, aided by spies and informers, and sustained by some churches, has resulted in an increased and increasing consumption of alcoholic drinks, and in one in fourteen of all the males between twenty-five and sixty becoming miserable drunkards.

The cause of this deplorable state of things is evident. The leaders of the movement have endeavored to repress rather than to confine and direct a natural desire. They have given us a new version of the story of those wise men of Gotham, who in order to capture a sparrow, built a wall around the tree on which it was perched, and were surprised to see it fly away at the conclusion of their labor. The only lull in the tide of drunkenness has been whenever and wherever malt liquors have supplanted distilled spirits in public use, and this substantial improvement the fanatical agitators have made the most herculean efforts to prevent.

The learned author of *Die Narkotischen Genussmittel und der Mensch* estimates that matè is used by ten millions of people; coca by as many more; chicory by forty millions; the chocolate bean by fifty millions; coffee and betel each by a hundred millions; hasheesh by three hundred millions; opium by four hundred millions; tea by five hundred millions; and tobacco by eight hundred millions. He might have added that, assuming the population of the globe to be one thousand millions, at least nine hundred millions use some kind of alcoholic stimulants. A practice so general, commencing in remote antiquity, common to both savage and civilized peoples, and resisting the sneers of the cynic and the remonstrance of the philanthropist, necessarily arises from a natural craving of man, and is one of those instincts which the wise statesman seeks to guide into the safest channels. The fanatic who attempts to abolish its use is certain to fail; the practical man who endeavors to prevent its abuse may succeed; when the frightful consequences of the crime of drunkenness and its effects on private health and public morals are considered, they become of the deepest interest; and the problem of the suppression of the abuse of stimulants one that requires the best powers of the wise and thoughtful for its true solution.

The demand of the human system for stimulants is not only natural but proper. For a stimulant is that substance which nourishes, or renders more easy the nourishing of the nervous system; and is demanded when the nerves are unduly taxed by mental or physical action. As all stimulants, from table salt to brandy, act in excess as narcotic poisons, by disturbing and paralyzing the nervous centres, most persons confound their narcotic effects with stimulation, which is a dangerous mistake. This error is one of the causes of excess. A person finds that a glass of wine, or a mug of ale, after his meals facilitates digestion, and renders him more cheerful thereby, or relieves him after a mental or physical strain. He may repeat it, or increase it in moderation to his advantage, and the only gauge of that moderation is experience; but if he take so much as to produce a forced and marked exhilaration of spirits, or a confused mental action, he is in the first stage of drunkenness, though all around may believe him to be perfectly sober. The desire for an occasional stimulant in its true meaning, is a proper craving of nature; and when we consider its true office, it is no wonder that nine out of ten people in the world indulge in alcoholic stimulants in some form, at one time or other.

Who began the use of fermented liquors—for distillation is comparatively a modern process—it is impossible to say. The earliest historical records show their general use. The Egyptians had their beer, and the Greeks, besides their grape wine, had their wine of barley, the *ek koithon methu* of Aischylos, and the *oinos koithonos* of Xenophon. It is possible that the dweller in the bone cavern used some product of fermentation to cheer his miserable existence, and the nomadic tribes merely continued the custom of their ancestors. The beer of the earliest periods, like the ale of England before the seventeenth century, was made without hops, and was probably something like the fermented drink now known as weiss beer. But whenever the use began it had an early beginning. All substances containing sugar, or starch capable of being converted to sugar, became the basis of fermented drinks. In countries where the grape flourished, wine was the result of the process; in less genial climes the farinaceous grains were used to manufacture beer. As knowledge spread, and taste grew refined, it became an object to find a drink that in moderation would stimulate and refresh, while it produced the least evil consequences when some drink-glutton indulged to excess. Experience at least taught that the fermented decoction of malted barley, clarified and preserved by the hop, best fulfilled these conditions. All the farinaceous grains are capable of the malting process, and one of them—maize or Indian corn—is particularly rich in starch; but barley malt is usually preferred.

Though it requires skill and experience to carry it out, the process of brewing is simple. The barley is prepared by the maltster, who brings it by moisture to the germinating point, where the starch is partially changed to sugar, and diastase, a nitrogenous substance having the power by its presence to change the farinaceous portions of the grain to glucose, is developed; and farther germination is then arrested by heat. This malt is bruised by the brewer, and placed in the mash-tub with warm water, which dissolves the sugar and diastase. The latter acting on the remainder of the starch, converts it to a gummy substance called dextrine, and grape sugar, and at last entirely into the latter substance. The infusion thus made is technically known as the wort. The quantity of diastase evolved is sufficient to convert into sugar ten times as much starch as is found in the malt, and the brewer could add the deficient amount to advantage; but, so far as I have observed, this is rarely, if ever, done in this country.

The next step in the process is to stop the action of the diastase when it has sufficiently performed its office, and this is done by boiling. The same heat coagulates the albumen, and extracts the aroma and bitterness of the hop, which is added at this stage. The time of boiling, its duration and the quantity of hops used, are determined by the skill and experience of the brewer, and have no arbitrary standard.

The boiled and hopped wort is now suffered to run into shallow receivers, where it is cooled as quickly as possible to a temperature most favorable to fermentation, which runs from 34 to 60 degrees of the Fahrenheit scale. When lowered to this, it is passed to the fermenting-tun; yeast, preferably from the variety of beer or ale to be made, is added, and it is allowed to ferment for about a week. Here from 50 to 75 per centum of the grape sugar is changed to alcohol—the remaining portion of the sugar being purposely left undecomposed, to prevent it from passing into the acetous fermentation, and as a foundation for additional carbonic dioxide—and the beer or ale is now ready to be stored in casks for preservation.

Such, divested of minor detail, is essentially the mode of manufacture. Now for the chemical action involved in the process.

Every one is familiar with starch and with cane sugar. But grape sugar, which belongs to the family of glucoses, is not so well known. It differs not only in appearance but in composition from the sugar of commerce and daily use. Like starch and the sucroses and alcohol, it contains carbon, hydrogen and oxygen, but not nitrogen. All these compounds of carbon and water—for the hydrogen and oxygen in all of them exist in the proportions to form water—are a necessary part of aliment; but they are heat-food, as the nitrogenous substances are flesh-food, and the one is as needful as the other. Though they may not repair, they retard the loss of tissue, and they furnish external fuel for that process of combustion in the human body which is commonly known as life.

When diastase, which is nitrogenous, is brought into contact with starch in solution, the latter imbibes no part of the nitrogen present, but at once begins to decompose, and to re-organize its constituents into two other compounds: namely, dextrine and grape sugar. The starch is made up of carbon 18 parts, hydrogen, 30, and oxygen, 15; and the water in which it is dissolved, of hydrogen, 2, and oxygen, 1. These amounts re-appear in dextrine, containing carbon, 12 parts, hydrogen, 20, and oxygen, 10; and grape sugar, with carbon, 6 parts, hydrogen, 12, and oxygen, 6; or, to put it in chemical formula, the initial letters of the elements forming the symbols, thus:

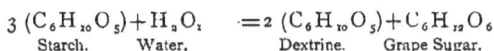

$$3 \ (C_6H_{10}O_5) + H_2O_1 \quad = 2 \ (C_6H_{10}O_5) + C_6H_{12}O_6$$

Starch.   Water.   Dextrine.   Grape Sugar.

Nothing is lost in this operation. Every element is present, and the sum of these elements is the same, but they re-appear in different combinations.

When fermentation is produced by the presence of yeast, or any other nitrogenous substance capable of provoking it, the sugar is decomposed, and the elements are recombined in two other substances: namely, the ethylic hydrate known as alcohol, and carbonic dioxide, formerly termed carbonic acid gas. The 6 parts of carbon, 12 of hydrogen, and 6 of oxygen, which constitute grape sugar, re-arrange themselves into alcohol which contains carbon, 4 parts, hydrogen, 12, and oxygen, 2; and carbonic dioxide, made up of carbon, 2 parts, and oxygen, 4; all of the former remaining in the beer with the unchanged sugar, gluten, and other extractive, while a part of the latter escapes, and the rest remains in the liquor to give it sparkle and piquancy. Chemically expressed, we have:

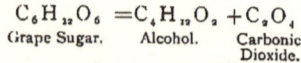

$$C_6H_{12}O_6 = C_4H_{12}O_2 + C_2O_4$$

Grape Sugar.   Alcohol.   Carbonic Dioxide.

The amount of alcohol in malt liquors varies according to the kind produced, from 1.26 per centum in small beer, to 8, or upward, in the stronger ales.

But alcohol is by no means the only substance held in solution or suspension in the beers. It is to the other substances we must look in order to see all the effects of malt liquors on the human system, and to explain why the action of alcohol in their case is so distinctly modified. Beer contains, besides the alcohol and carbonic dioxides, unchanged grape sugar, gluten, and a trifle of mineral matter from the grain, with some of the aromatic resin, the bitter or tonic principle, and a minute portion of the volatile oil—the greater part of this last having been dissipated by boiling—of the hop. Then there is a very small quantity of tannic acid, which aids to clarify the beer, and sometimes a trace of acetic acid. The amount of extractive matter varies; but in a properly prepared beer it is in proportion to the amount of alcohol present. It may be as low as 1.5 per centum, or as high as 10, or more,—some of the German beers, not fully fermented, containing from 10 to 12, and Burton ale, 12.47, both being nearly as rich in gluten as cow's milk. It is upon the amount and character of this extract that the nutritive force of the beer mainly depends, as the stimulating effect does on the alcohol, and the grateful sensation to the palate on the carbonic dioxide. The first furnishes a nutritive substance easily assimilated, while the second facilitates digestion, aids nutrition, and retards the waste of tissue, and the latter refreshes the nerves of taste.

The part played by alcohol, in moderate amounts, in the human system, is misunderstood by many. Superficial observers are apt to think, because nitrogenous substances are flesh-forming food, that the only food proper to be taken is that which forms flesh. The deduction does not follow from the premises. Heat-formers are equally necessary as part of our aliment, and carbonaceous food, in the shape of starch, sugar or alcohol, are equally required on the diet-list,—the preference being given to one or the other, according to the circumstances of the case. Nor is it an objection to a stimulant that, if excessively used, it acts as a narcotic. The *theine* of tea, and the *caffeine* of coffee, in excess, paralyze the nervous centres. The peculiar effects of a strong and concentrated dose of tea or coffee on the heart and brain are well known, and are doubtless due to their active principles. But tea and coffee, moderately used, are beneficial. They not only soothe the system, and produce a cheerful frame of mind, followed by no depression, but they retard the change of matter going on in the body, and diminish waste,—thus, indirectly, assisting nutrition. Alcohol does more. It retards waste still more strongly, giving to the system a part of the carbon and oxygen thrown off by the breath, and which constitutes the greater part of loss in life-combustion. If it, indeed, produced stimulation alone, it would be worthy of note and moderate use. It is an error to suppose that man exists merely to appease hunger and slake thirst in the intervals of toil and sleep. He is gifted with instincts, cravings, sentiments and passions that are made to be satisfied to a reasonable extent. A love of stimulants seems to be inherent, and is gratified in some shape or other by nearly every one of mature age, whether he does it openly or surreptitiously,—whether he take his beer, his wine, or his ardent spirits, or whether he indulge in tea, coffee, or root-beer.

In a moderate quantity, pure malt liquor adds to cheerfulness of spirit, soothes the nerves, gives tone to the system, and improves the general health. They are used medically in certain diseases where there is a low state of the system, but principally during convalescence from diseases which have weakened the body, and impaired the physical powers. In some cases they are contra-indicated; but those are a matter for the judgment of the physician. In excess, it produces injury, as all stimulants do when pushed to the degree of narcotism. The wine-sot is liable to gout and apoplexy ; the gin-sot to kidney-disease; the brandy-sot to liver-disease and *delirium tremens*, in which the whiskey-sot shares ; the tea-sot to nervous disorder; the coffee-sot to softening of the spinal marrow ; the water-sot, for there be such things as water-sots, to hypochondriasis, anæmia, and preternatural waste of tissue; and the beer-sot to unhealthy accumulations of fat on the viscera, and disorder of the serous membranes. A moderate amount of malt liquor—and moderation is a relative term—agrees with most people, and is beneficial in every way. But there are exceptions. There are some persons to whom malt liquor is injurious, just as there are some to whom wine, even of the lighter kinds, is poisonous; and others whose nervous system seems to be unhappily affected by a single cup of tea. On the other hand, I have known men who lived to a good old age, in excellent health, and yet drank daily quantities of malt liquors that would have narcotized most persons fearfully. Even whiskey, wherein the alcohol is modified by the ethers and water only, is borne by some persons in quantities that set all theory at defiance. In my own neighborhood, I knew an old gentleman who lived to the last in vigorous health, was always sober and decorous, and who died between the age of ninety-nine and a hundred. He told me once that he had drank enough apple-jack in his time to have floated a ship, and assured me that a pint of that drink, in the twenty-four hours, was a moderate allowance for a healthy man. But these are puzzling exceptions, and do not disprove that moderation in amount is requisite in general. A comparison with wine-drinkers, tea-drinkers, and water-drinkers, is favorable to the consumer of malt liquors, in health, comfort, and length of life. The records of disease, and the bills of mortality, in beer-drinking countries display a less percentage of sickness, and longer lives, than in other countries where malt liquors are replaced by other beverages,—unless, indeed, the stories of so many men of extreme old age in Russia are to be credited, and that *quass* and brandy-drinking country be an exception.

It is frequently said, and repeated as though the reiteration were proof, that malt liquors must be injurious from the alcohol they contain, since alcohol in a sufficient dose and undiluted will destroy life, and that alcohol undergoes no change in the system, but is eliminated in the same state as when it entered; and the crude philosophers who make these assertions cite experiments made in glass tubes to show that alcohol destroys the gastric juice, that it preserves dead flesh, and therefore must impede digestion, with a great many other assertions of the kind, most of which are untrue, and others by no means sustaining the general deduction. It does not follow that a substance which, in its unmodified or absolute state, may, in a sufficient quantity destroy life, must necessarily be injurious when modified by its combinations, and taken in moderate quantities. The active principles of a number of refreshing and healthful substances are virulent poisons. The citric acid of lemon juice, the acetic acid of vinegar, the sodium and the chlorine of table salt, the theine of tea, the caffeine of coffee—all these are capable of destroying life effectually; but the value of the substances in which they are found is recognized by science and the experience of common life. In them, as in malt liquors, the poisonous principle is modified by the combinations. In the case of the air we breathe we have a still more striking example. This is a mere mechanical mixture of two deadly poisons—the nitrogen exists not as an oxide, but in an unchanged state, yet we breathe it with impunity, and could not get along without it. Rob air of its oxygen and we would soon die, the human system would expire from lack of the means of combustion; divest it of its nitrogen, and the human system would burn itself out speedily. There is no evidence that alcohol, when combined with water and nutritive substances, as in the case of malt liquors, undergoes no change in the stomach, but just the reverse. The experiments made in glass tubes have no practical value until human digestion is carried on in that kind of vessels. The experiments on the human stomach, to be satisfactory, must ḅe carried on in the stomach. That a small glass of brandy does assist digestion, probably by exciting an additional flow of gastric juice, is the experience of many a glutton, who finds the horrors of indigestion relieved in that way. The mere fact that alcohol will preserve unchewed dead flesh is not proof that it impedes digestion, or remains unchanged in the human system. Gastric juice will preserve meat in the same way. Let these experimenters take flesh, thoroughly chewed, masticated by the teeth, properly comminuted and mingled with the saliva, and place it with ale, in a glass tube, and keep it at the average heat of the stomach, and report the result. Let some of them take too much sugar in their stomach and observe the acetous eructations and extra carbonic dioxide that come from the stomach, and not from the lungs, in due course of time. A part of the sugar has been changed to vinegar, and no acetous fermentation can take place without being preceded by the alcoholic. In fact the beer-glutton is frequently troubled with those very fumes, which uncomfortably demonstrate to the sot that the alcohol in the beer has undergone a very striking and unpleasant change in the system.

Much has been said about the adulteration of malt liquors. It is quite common to hear total abstinence speakers, and read total abstinence writers, who speak or write of the difficulty of procuring a genuine glass of ale, and mourn the matter in a pathetic way that should only be expected of a devoted beer-drinker. Common sense should show that men engaged in an occupation involving a large outlay of capital, and in a business whose success depends upon the purity of a product submitted to thousands of critical judges, and with natural rivals in trade around, are not apt to risk loss by tricks of this kind, even if they were not men of good character and unblemished reputations, as the leading brewers certainly are. The total abstinence men have recently brought chemistry to aid common sense on this point. There lies before me a pamphlet called "The History and Mystery of a Glass of Ale," by T. W. Kirton, published by " The National Temperance Society and Publishing House." In this the author insinuates that strychnia—*credat Judæus apella*—is used as a cheaper thing than hops to give bitterness to malt liquors, and that alum, copperas, *cocculus indicus*, tobacco and salt, are necessary ingredients in the beers. In the same tract, however, we are treated to analyses by Professor Chandler, of New-York City, of five different makes of lager-beer, in which the amount of alcohol and extractive are given, doubtless, with commendable accuracy. But this work, done in the interest of the temperance agitators, seems to have been too accurately performed; for the statement concludes with the following words, inadvertently printed with the rest, and the antidote thus given with the bane:—"A most thorough examination failed to reveal any indication of the presence of picric acid, picrotoxine (the peculiar principle of *cocculus indicus*), of alum, copperas, or any other adulteration whatever." The chemist had evidently set out to look for this adulteration, and he found it, not in the beer, but in the imagination of Mr. Kirton and his comrades.

The effect of the consumption of malt liquors on public morals can only be determined by a careful examination of the character of the various nations where they form the popular drink. Statistics are not always trustworthy, for the science of statistics is yet in its infancy, and entire accuracy is impossible. So far as we can ascertain them, the facts are in favor of the beer-drinkers—the morals of that part of Bavaria where beer is produced to the amount of 2 or 4 hectolitres per head, and the greater part consumed at home, comparing favorably with those of the State of Maine, where the amount brewed is a trifle, and the amount consumed probably less, —for a prohibitory law enforced by public opinion is able to drive away a bulky substance like malt liquor, though powerless against the more portable distilled spirits. The percentage of convictions for crimes in the beer-drinking parts of Germany, where the law is enforced with known strictness, is much less than in countries using other kinds of drinks; as may be readily seen by reference to the record. Drunkenness and breaches of the peace are comparatively rare there. Even in parts of the same country the consumption of beer seems to be in ratio to good order. Thus in Posen, where the consumption is at the rate of less than nine quarts per head per annum, there is more drunkenness than in Berlin, where it reached as high as ninety-five quarts per annum. Certainly the morals of Germany, by the concurrent testimony of travelers and the official records, its public order, its social happiness, and its standard of right, do not suffer in comparison with those of Italy, where beer is almost unknown, or those of Turkey, where fermented liquors are forbidden by law and religion.

The prosperity and intellectual progress of a people, are important matters to be considered in connection with the beverages they use. We are told by total abstinence writers that two-thirds of the pauperism of the world is caused by intemperance, and I am willing, for one, to credit this statement. It may be interesting, therefore, to continue the contrast of Bavaria, the beer-drinking country *par eminence*, with that of Maine, the total abstinence State *par excellence*, in this matter. The advantages or disadvantages in the struggle for subsistence are about the same in amount in both States, though differing in character. In Bavaria, society is old, habit strong, the fetters of trade not easily broken, untilled land scarce, and population dense. In Maine, there is abundance of new land, much timber unconsumed, no limits on a choice of occupation, comparatively a new society, and a sparse population. The men of Maine have just that uncongenial climate which stimulates to industry, and pique themselves on their energy. Yet in Bavaria, few receive aid from the State or the municipality; while in Maine, the record in this respect is frightful. By the census of 1870, we find that the State of Maine had one person in every 172.65 a pauper, while the pauper rate of the whole Union was only one in 502.47. Bavaria, in spite of emigration, increased her population .70 per centum during the last census decade, while Maine, the only one of the United States in the same category, decreased her population, .34 per centum. Judging by the result, the driving out of beer by pains and penalties must have driven the men of Maine to an enormous amount of illicit whiskey-drinking, and consequent intemperance; and we may readily credit the assertion of travelers, who say that no one need go without his dram of whiskey in Maine, though a glass of beer is not to be had for love or money. The general decrease of pauperism in the United States during the decade when the production of beer rose from over a million of barrels per annum, to over eight millions of barrels, is a significant fact. In 1860, the average number of paupers in the United States was one in 379.09. In 1870, this had fallen to one in 502.47. And it might be well for legislators and others to consider the connection between the proverbial thrift of the German immigrant here, and his indulgence in beer. As for the intellectual advance of the beer-drinking countries compared to others, it is so notorious as to need no elucidation here.

· Now, no one claims that there is any panacea in beer for moral ills or financial disaster. But in the recent attacks upon the use of malt liquors, the total abstinence men assume that the use of beer "demoralizes" men, deteriorates the race, and produces pauperism and crime, and is a bar to intellectual progress and religious sentiments. An inspection of the record shows this charge to be untrue, and if we are to rely upon the most carefully gathered statistics, the contrary would be the natural inference. The progress of the beer-drinking nations of Europe in civilization, letters, morals, and good government, is in no wise inferior to those countries where wine or whiskey is the national drink, and they shine in all these things with the solitary State where it is said cold water reigns supreme, and men are abstinent by operation of law. What I claim in this matter is, first, that man will use stimulants; secondly, that, from the weakness of human nature, he is prone to use them in excess; thirdly, that the stimulant which, when pushed to narcotism, contains the least modicum of injurious substances, combined with the greatest amount of nutritive matter, should be preferably encouraged; fourthly, that the evils of drunkenness are only averted by teaching men, from their infancy, the nature and effects of stimulants and narcotics on the system, and not by empty declamation, unfounded assertions, virulent abuse, and powerless statutes. No man has a right to make his own action the standard of a community. I have no fondness for malt liquors; for whiskey I have a dislike, and for gin an aversion. Yet I have no desire to impose my tastes and distastes on my neighbors, to whom either of these drinks may be pleasant, and, in moderation, healthful. If they exceed the proper amount, and so lay themselves open to punishment, they should be dealt with as any other law-breakers. I have had during my life many opportunities for observation, professionally and otherwise. I have been called to attend sick men who were beer-drinkers, whiskey-drinkers, and water-drinkers. I have observed the advantages and disadvantages of the habits of each, and I have come to the conclusion that, while the water-drinker escapes delirium tremens and gout, he is more liable to pulmonary diseases, and the disorders arising from defective nutrition, than those who use alcoholic drinks in moderation, and that his only safety, in many instances, lies in those very liquids which he holds in aversion. Of course this statement will be tortured by unscrupulous fellows into something else, and they will unblushingly say that I am pleading for intemperance. But that will be on a par with the false statistics and extravagant statements sent through the country of late years on this subject. The records show that the crusade against malt liquors has no foundation in sense or fact; that their consumption has increased everywhere *pari passu* with the increase of health, comfort, civilization and intellectual advance, and that to repress their use by legislation or prejudice, is to throw back the mass to more dangerous beverages, and so inflict a deadly blow on the well-being of society.

The Americans, on the whole, are a practical people. Whatever fools or fanatics may do or say, the mass of our population are not apt to continue in any course of action which does not attain a desired end. Drunkenness is a great evil. Its results are most deplorable. Any right course of action that will diminish it, and if possible repress it, should be aided and encouraged by every good citizen. But all efforts in that direction must be based on common sense, and those who make them must ac-

cept the lessons of experience. That a powerful organization of zealous and enthu-
siastic people, aided by a supposed popular sentiment, and sustained by a number
of religious sects, has not only failed to extirpate the crime and folly of drunkenness,
after a crusade extending over so many years, but have seen it increase, as they assert,
is a fact showing conclusively that there is something unwise in their course of action,
or that the action itself is injudicious. When a real practical mode of diminishing
the tendency to excess is indicated,—when any reasonable mode, differing from that
which has so signally failed, is suggested,—is it not their duty to give it a fair trial?
That is a question to be answered by sober and practical men, and not by those who
are drunken with fanaticism, and who mistake false figures for statistics, and empty
assertion for logical argument. It is a question to be determined by a careful consideration of the circumstances of the case, and the character of our people. If it be
impossible to prevent the use of alcoholic stimulants, and the experience of all mankind and all time proves it, would it not be a solid gain to temperate living to substitute the weaker for the stronger beverages? The total abstinence men, it seems to
me, have gone to work at the wrong end of their task. They have striven to cut off
the supply, without diminishing the demand, and thus brought in their way the bar of
an inevitable law of trade. Their first business should be to educate the mass in
regard to the effects of intoxicating drinks, and the effects of pushing the use of
stimulants to the point of narcotism. If they even succeed in substituting the milder
for the stronger drinks meanwhile, they have gained something. But against these
they exhibit the most virulence. They aid distilled spirits by indirection. Is it possible that they fear the loss of "frightful examples," should men betake themselves to
the products of the brewery and wine-press, rather than to those of the still? They
need have no apprehension on that score. There will be always fools who will get
drunk, even if they have to resort to those pernicious alcoholic drinks, currant wine,
or root beer, for the purpose. Or is it the fever of madness that impels them to the
worst mode of doing the best thing, and renders them deaf to reason and blind
to facts? Fortunately the solution of this matter does not rest with them, but with
those who are sober in thought, and temperate in action. In spite of their frantic
folly, drunkenness has really decreased relatively to the population; and though greater
quantities of alcoholic stimulants are consumed, they are of a less potent nature
than before. Individuals do not consume more malt liquors per head, but more individuals use malt liquors, and this distinction, which embodies an important difference,
is all the better for the health, morals, and prosperity of the country.

OPINIONS AND FACTS FROM EMINENT PHYSICIANS, CHEMISTS, AND OTHERS, IN FAVOR OF ALE AND BEER AS LIGHT, WHOLESOME BEVERAGES.

THE following pages are submitted to the public in the belief that a perusal of the conclusive evidence recorded in them, cannot fail to convince any unprejudiced readers of the usefulness and value of malt liquors as light, wholesome beverages for the people.

All the writings from which extracts have been made are by the very highest authorities on this subject. They are from men eminent in their different branches of science, from whom all persons are glad to receive professional advice on other subjects connected with the general health of the community. And the unanimity of opinions and conclusions reached by these authors, generally in entire ignorance of each other's writings, is certainly remarkable.

These extracts are submitted without comments, as they speak for themselves; and it is hoped that they will be read by all, whether at present favorably or unfavorably disposed toward the further introduction of ale and beer.

FROM THE ANNUAL REPORT OF THE STATE BOARD OF HEALTH OF MASSACHUSETTS FOR 1872.

"*Alcoholic Drinks.—Their Use and Abuse.—Analysis of the Information derived from Correspondence throughout the Globe.* (By the CHAIRMAN, DR. HENRY I. BOWDITCH.) The Board submits to the Legislature this paper prepared with care and labor by the Chairman. The Board presents it as a valuable contribution to the discussion of the general subject of the use and effect of intoxicating drink."

"OCTOBER 15, 1871.

"*To the Members of the Massachusetts State Board of Health.*

"GENTLEMEN: In our Second Annual Report is printed a correspondence on the use and abuse of alcoholic stimulants among foreign nations, and a comparison of the same with our own country in this particular. I think this correspondence is unique, not only for the extent of the surface of the globe that it embraces, but likewise for the character of our correspondents.

"I have thought that they should receive attention from us, and that all their essential truths or apparent truths should be sifted out and brought more clearly into view. I have had this end in view while preparing this communication for you; and I trust you will believe that I have endeavored to get at the exact truth.

"In commencing the correspondence as your representative, I had no other object in view than to get the opinions of able correspondents, most of them either American ambassadors to different courts, or consuls from the American government, stationed in all the various important countries of the world to which our commerce extends. My questions embraced two main ideas. They were put briefly, because I believed that if I asked a few questions containing seminal principles, I should get ampler responses than if I should ask a greater nnmber, which would necessarily require a longer time, and perhaps much study, to answer correctly.

"The papers were sent to thirty-three resident American ambassadors, and one hundred and thirty-two consuls, and a few other non-official personages and friends, whose opinions I knew would be of great value, if obtained.

"Among these correspondents are many of our most distinguished citizens, some of whom are well known for their eminent intellectual and moral qualities. Usually they have resided for some years in the places from which they write, and are, of course, generally well acquainted with the habits of the people, not only of the cities from which they reply, but also with those of the people of the districts or countries in which these cities are situated. Most of them write as if they knew well the habits of the people, and also those of our own nation, in reference to the use and abuse of stimulating drink. Hence their opinions on that subject are of great value.

"*Love of Stimulants a Human Instinct.*—The first deduction we can make from this correspondence is, that this appetite for stimulants is one of the strongest of human instincts. It is seen in every nation, in all quarters of the globe. Savage or civilized man alike purchases or makes his appropriate stimulant. Nature seems, in fact, unbounded in its liberality in this particular; for, wherever on the globe he may be, man finds some means for exhilaration or for soothing himself amid the cares and trials that he may meet. Having been made a free agent, he is permitted to use or abuse this bounty, and his own tendency to drink.

"*Legislators cannot neglect these great Cosmic and Social Laws.*—In all his dealings with intemperance in this country, the real statesman *must* consider these primal influences of the climate in which a people lives, and of these tastes of the race. In our country, the question is presented in a more complicated form than in any other, from the very fact of the great variety of people that forms our nation. Doubtless this makes legislation more difficult; but that is no reason why a statesman should ignore these great facts.

"*Are all kinds of Ales, Beer, Rum, and distilled Alcoholic Stimulants to be classed as alike equally and always injurious?*—Some writers in this country and in Europe, in their zeal for the noble cause of temperance, take the affirmative of this question, and claim that alcohol in any form is '*always a poison.*' I cannot hold this opinion, nor do I think that the clinical experience of any physician will admit of it.

" I believe that physicians do at times save human life by using various stimulating drinks with the utmost freedom. Moreover, I do not believe there is a single article in the *materia medica*, that in its various forms of elixirs, tinctures, extracts, etc., or when simply combined with water, is more necessary than alcohol in the treatment of disease. I know that some excellent friends claim that some time in the future ' good times' something will be found that will supersede the use of alcohol. They hope for this, believing as they do that it is always ' a poison;' but, even while they assert this, they use these very poisons in their daily practice. I think there are but very few, if any, who are confident that *they* will ever see the time when they will be able to give up such use.

" It is well for us all to deal frankly on this subject. It is time now to look at this question fairly and simply. I take the following position; and I fearlessly assert that clinical experience proves, if it prove anything, that every form of stimulant now in use can be made a blessing, if used temperately and on proper occasions. But I likewise most freely admit, that, if used intemperately and improperly, each and all may become ' poisonous' to the last degree. Yet more, I believe that, even when used intemperately, light beer, ale, lager-beer, wines like claret, etc., do vastly less harm than the stronger ardent spirits. In truth, the former cannot produce intoxication, except after the swallowing of a very large quantity,—so large, that, before intoxication is produced, the disposition to drink is satiated.

" There is no doubt that the American people, as a whole, do not by any means as yet understand the true philosophy of food and drink; and this opinion, held by many, and which has been the basis of State legislation for years past, viz., that *all* liquors are in themselves nothing but evil, and equally evil if once taken into the human stomach, proves the truth of this assertion. It is radically and wholly erroneous. Those who claim to be the especial apostles of temperance say, that every one who drinks at dinner a glass of lager-beer sets quite as bad an example as the most incorrigible drunkard. In drinking even thus moderately, 'temperately,' he proves that he does not believe that alcohol under every form and at all times is a '*poison*,' and therefore to be absolutely and at all times even in the smallest quantities prohibited.

" *Intemperance as it may be hereafter influenced by the Cultivation of the Grape, and by the making and using of mild native Wines and of Lager-Beer.—Grape Culture and Lager-Beer in America.*—It is the general view presented by our correspondence, that in the wine-making districts of Europe intoxication is less frequent and less severe than in our country. Unfortunately we have never *extensively* cultivated the grape with the idea of making wines.

" I fully agree with all that has been said of the value of light wines as an aid to temperance; but I believe that Germans are destined to be really the greatest benefactors of this country, by bringing to us, if we choose to accept the boon, their beer. Lager-beer contains less alcohol than any of the native grape wines. This fact, with the other fact, that the Germans have not the pernicious habits of our people, would, if we chose to adopt their customs, tend to diminish intemperance in this country.

" *What shall we do in Massachusetts to prevent the Evil of a too free Use of Intoxicating Drinks, and to make our People truly Temperate?*—I am confident that our people could be gradually led to a higher temperance by appeals to common sense, while depicting the evils of intemperance, by observing that the use of some liquors is deleterious, while the '*temperate*' use of others does little or no harm.

" It is much to be regretted that there is, at present, no common ground of temperance permitted to exist by the ultra defenders of *either* side of this important question. Some desire total abstinence to be the rule. On the other hand, this idea is resisted by many with an energy which threatens to lead to the *opposite* extreme of perfect freedom in the sale of all intoxicating drinks. But the larger proportion of the community, while working and praying for temperance, do nevertheless use, and feel that they have a perfect right to use, wine or ale, if not for good companionship, at least for the reason St. Paul advised Timothy to use it; viz., for ' thy stomach's sake.' Under the banner of total abstinence from all stimulating drinks these latter persons cannot stand. They are *temperate* drinkers, and therefore cannot be received as comrades among those who claim to be the only true defenders of the temperance faith. Let us look a little more closely into this subject of intoxicating, stimulating articles. Alcohol is not by any means the only stimulus that brings disease and misery on human beings.

" Were, therefore, a strict rule made, that no article stimulating to the nervous system should be used by the present party of devotees to abstinence, the dogma would split that party into innumerable fragments. It would probably be divided into various small cliques, each excluded for its intemperate use of some favorite stimulus,—tobacco, opium, coffee, or tea, etc. Scarcely a week passes that I am not called to '*prohibit*,' in a particular case, all use of the one or the other of these articles.

" If the community follow the extremists of either side, a common standing-spot can never be found. It is evident, if we can trust human testimony as given by our correspondents, beers and mild native wines should appear in a very different light before us from that which ardent spirits should hold. Cannot *Total Abstinence* advocates, therefore, as a present *Temperance measure*, permit the use of beer and light wines ? Can there not be a union on this reasonable basis ?

" My position will be opposed by many. It will be denied that this is a human instinct ; and, in proof, it may be said that some men, and more women, never, during their whole lives, use stimulants. Before admitting this argument, I must ask how many there are in the world who do not *use some stimulant*. There may be many who do not use alcoholic stimulants ; but I suspect that there are but few, almost none, who ' totally abstain ' from *all* stimulants, unless, perchance, it be some anchorite in his mountain cell, who, from fanaticism, chooses to eat pulse and to drink water. I deem a love of stimulants as much a human instinct as any other of the so-called human instincts. And the proposition of total abstinence from stimulants, because intoxication prevails widely in the community, seems to me as preposterous as it would be to advise universal celibacy, because of the existence of gross evils in connection with those instincts that lead to the divine institution of marriage.

" From the study I have made of our correspondence, I am induced to believe that the permission to sell mild ales, beer, and light wines, would, under certain very general rules, be really a promotion of temperance in New England, as it apparently is elsewhere.

" Beer, native light grape wines, and ardent spirits should not be classed together ; for they produce very different effects on the individual and upon the race.

" Light German beer and ale can be used even freely without any very apparent injury to the individual, or without causing intoxication. They contain very small percentages of alcohol (4 or 4.5 to 6.50 per cent.).

" By classifying all liquors as equally injurious, and by endeavoring to further that idea in the community, are we not doing a real injury to the country by preventing a freer use of a mild beer, or of native grape wine, instead of the ardent spirits to which our people are now so addicted ?

" In the sincere belief, gentlemen, that this analysis of our correspondence will, eventually at least, tend to help onward the most excellent cause of temperance everywhere, and in the hope that none will be offended at the expression, at times, of my own individual opinions, which, in the course of the discussion, I have deemed it my right and duty to give, I remain,

" Your colleague and friend,

" HENRY I. BOWDITCH."

EXTRACTS FROM THE CORRESPONDENCE REFERRED TO BY DR. BOWDITCH.

LETTER FROM A PHYSICIAN IN MASSACHUSETTS.

" I should, however, make a distinction between the use of intoxicating liquors and the lighter drinks. If we could so manage as to furnish the people with light wines, lager-beer, and such drinks, and dispense with distilled liquors, I believe that the community would be immensely benefited."

LETTER FROM ANOTHER PHYSICIAN IN MASSACHUSETTS.

" I have had a very large practice among the Germans for twenty years; and my observation has been, that they are remarkably free from consumption and chronic diseases. I have attributed it to their free use of lager-beer. I believe that the moderate use of the lighter drinks is beneficial."

" CONSULATE-GENERAL OF THE UNITED STATES,
FRANKFORT-ON-THE-MAIN, May 20, 1870.

" Such was the state twenty years ago. By the improvements in making better beer, things have changed. The drunkards have disappeared. A great deal less of cider and wine is consumed. The people now generally drink beer. Intoxication has decreased. . . . .

" It cannot be said that the general health of the people suffers in this part of Germany. In the city of Frankfort, with a population of one hundred thousand persons, and an average annual mortality of fifteen hundred persons, hardly an average of five persons have died of delirium tremens."

" UNITED STATES LEGATION, VIENNA,
June 17, 1870.

" I am advised by those in whose judgment I have confidence, that the chief intoxicating drinks in Austria are beer and wine, and that but comparatively a small amount of spirituous liquors is consumed, excepting in Galicia.

" Touching the relative amount of intoxication in the country where I am residing, and that seen in the United States, I may say that I have seen more intoxicated persons in the streets of New York in one day than I have chanced to see in Vienna during the past year. " I am, sir, very respectfully yours,

"JOHN JAY."

" A physician, who has under his professional charge a large institution for the maintenance of aged persons, informs us that the demand among the inmates for stimulus in the form of tea is a matter of constant observation; and he moreover gives it as his opinion, that from twenty to twenty-five per cent. of the whole number are *tea-sots*, drinking tea regularly from four to six times daily, and as much oftener as they can procure it. They show the effect of this over-stimulation by increased mental irritability, muscular tremors; also in a greater or less degree by sleeplessness.

" The following fact has also come to our knowledge : A domestic in the family of a friend appeared at times intoxicated. As it was certain she could not get any of the so-called intoxicating liquors, great surprise was caused, until at length the problem was solved by the discovery that the individual drank large quantities of the strongest tea, of which she was constantly sipping."

FROM THE STATE BOARD OF HEALTH REPORT, 1872.

On the Use of Opium, by Dr. F. E. Oliver.

" The consideration of a remedy for this habit, if such there be, hardly falls within our province. We may, perhaps, be pardoned the suggestion, however, that based as it is upon a craving that no laws can eradicate, the allowance of those milder stimulants, everywhere in use in continental Europe, might aid at least in lessening the consumption of both alcohol and opium. It is an instructive fact, that in the history of legislation, whether against opium, alcohol, tobacco, or coffee,—for all have at different periods been the subjects of legislative enactment,—in no instance has the end sought been reached. Substitution or successful evasion has been the immediate consequence of all such efforts. In countries where the culture of the vine prevails, drunkenness and opium-eating are comparatively almost unknown. It is certainly not unreasonable to suppose that the permitted use of the lighter wines, and among malt wines of beer, would tend to the prevention of the latter habit, and in time go far toward solving the vexed question which of late seems to have disturbed the public mind."

LETTER OF JUSTUS VON LIEBIG, THE EMINENT GERMAN CHEMIST.

" In virtue of its characteristic ingredients, beer unites in its composition a number of conditions by which, in the human body, the consequences on the nervous system of the action of alcohol, which exalts the functions of the brain and spinal cord, are, after a certain time, more or less completely neutralized.

" Fermented juices in general differ from spirits in containing alkalies, organic acids, and certain other substances, which it is the business of chemistry more especially to ascertain.

" Fermented liquors, when taken with lean flesh and little bread, yield a diet approaching to milk, and with fat meat one approaching to rice or potatoes, in the relative proportions of plastic and non-nitrogenous constituents."

MALT LIQUORS—EXTRACT AND ALCOHOL—VALUE FOR FEEDING PURPOSES OF BREWERY "GRAINS," &c.; AND GENERAL STATISTICS.—By A. SCHWARZ.

AMONG all drinks, those as well which nature furnishes in abundance, as also those which are produced by human skill, beer especially commends itself by its properties as an excellent beverage. Milk contains nutritious substances (protein), and various salts; wine contains alcohol and small quantities of salts; the mineral waters, which render such valuable service to the diseased human organism, contain acids and salts; coffee and tea, volatile aromatic oils and alkaloids, and the strong, spirituous liquors, as whiskey, brandy, rum, arrac, and cognac, contain only more or less alcohol with some ethereal oils. The various other fancy and temperance drinks are distinguished only by their watery contents, which are flavored with sugar and extracts of plants and herbs to make them taste less insipid.

But beer contains protein, alcohol, salts, and carbonic acid gas, and, hence, possesses nutritious, stimulating, and refreshing properties. We do not intend to write a eulogy of beer, but only to state in its favor what cannot be denied by any man, be he a physician or a mechanic, a philosopher or a manufacturer, a chemist or an engineer, a wine-drinker or a temperance-man. We denote as *extract* of beer, those solid substances which are not, through the fermentation of the wort, transformed into volatile bodies, and therefore remain as a sediment after the evaporation of the beer. This extract consists of malt sugar, obtained by the mashing process, of albumen, contained in the malt and now dissolved, and of certain salts, especially phosphoric salt, which were originally contained in the barley, and have not been lost during the process of brewing.

The amount of the extract of beer mainly depends on the original concentration of the wort and on that state of fermentation in which the beer is consumed. It varies from 3 to 8 per cent. By virtue of its protein and its salts, it has a nutritious effect upon the human organism, and though it does so in a less degree than meat or bread, yet, on account of the form of solution in which it appears in the beer, it is easier assimilated, *i. e.*, it easily enters the organism, and plays a prominent part in the formation of milk, muscle, flesh and bones.

Good and wholesome meat contains in 100 parts:

Fibrine	17.5
Albumen	2.2
Extract by alcohol	1.5
" by water	1.3

Solid ingredients	22.5

As the fibrine cannot be taken in account in the process of nutrition, we must, in comparing the nutritious proportions of meat and beer, only consider the other ingredients of meat, which amount to 5 per cent. If we assume the amount of extract from the beer produced in the United States,—which, owing to the peculiar character of our barley and of our climatic conditions, attenuates abnormally,—to be in the average 4½ per cent., the 9,000,000 barrels of beer (to give it in a round sum) manufactured in the United States will yield 405,000 barrels or 81,000,000 lbs. of extract. According to the above statement, based on scientific investigation, this quantity of extract of beer represents 1,621,000,000 lbs. of beef.

Good cow's milk contains from 13 to 15 per cent. solid substances, hence 100 gallons will, in the average, yield 14 gallons of nutritious matter. Compared with milk the extract of beer produced and consumed in the United States represents annually 86,071,430 gallons of milk.

The amount of alcohol in beer depends on the decomposition of the extract originally contained in the wort, and is in proportion to the carbonic acid gas formed in the process.

We neither can nor wish to deny, that in consequence of containing alcohol, beer possesses intoxicating properties; but the quantity of alcohol contained in beer is so small, and so much diluted with water, that it can produce intoxication only if consumed in a great quantity, *i. e.*, by an immoderate use.

The percentage of alcohol in our lager-beer, ale and porter, varies from 4 to 7 per cent. Calculating from this statement, how much absolute alcohol is in one year consumed in beer throughout the United States, we find, that 9,000,000 barrels of beer, containing in the average 5.5 per cent. of alcohol, yield 495,000 barrels or 23,850,000 gallons of alcohol. *The State of Ohio produces in the whiskey manufactured there in one year more alcohol than is in all States of the Union put together, produced in one year in the beer they manufacture.*

Mr. Edward Young, at the head of the Office of Statistics at Washington, made a highly interesting estimate of the consumption of spirituous liquors in the United States for the year 1871. The amount expended for their consumption is, according to his statement, for—

Whiskey 60,000,000 gallons at $6 retail	$360,000,000
Imported spirits 2,500,000 gallons at $8	20,000,000
Ale, beer and porter, 6,500,000 bbls., at $20	130,000,000
Brandies, wines and liquors	31,500,000
Total	$541,500,000

The above mentioned prices represent retail figures, at such prices as liquor is generally sold at retail. The value of the above liquors, according to their production, would reduce the total amount one-half. According to these statements, which show the annual expense for whiskey to be $360,000,000, it is clear, that pauperism spreads mainly among the whiskey-drinking population, while those who drink beer consume a product which, in proportion to the amount of alcohol it contains, is more expensive, spend only $130,000,000 yearly, and at the same time imbibe a far smaller amount of alcohol.

The following chemical analysis of various kinds of lager-beer will give the best information concerning the extract and alcohol contained in them :

New York beer,	- - -	3.6	4.8	Newark, N. J. beer,	- -	3.2	5.4
" " "	- - -	4.4	3.7	Cincinnati, O. "	-	3.4	5.5
" " "	- - -	3.6	4.6	" " "	- -	4.0	5.7
" " "	- - -	4.2	5.3	Philadelphia, Pa."	- -	5.2	5.6

This pamphlet contains an article pointing to the enormous values annually represented by the production of the raw materials, barley and hops, necessary to the manufacture of beer. It is proved there, that thousands of workmen find profitable employment in malt-houses and breweries, and that millions of dollars are invested in this trade.

But the brewing business not only uses the products of agriculture and mining (coal), paying profitable prices for them, but it gives back to agriculture, in the so-called refuse, materials of inestimable worth. It does not only receive and take; it also gives and bestows.

In the beer breweries of the United States, are annually used about 25,000,000 bushels of malt. This yields about $2\frac{1}{2}$ per cent. " sprouts," or 625,000 bushels of sprouts.

We determine the value of the various kinds of fodder used for animals according to the amount of albumen contained in them, and for the comparison of the various values of fodder, agriculturists take that of hay as a unit. Sprouts contain from 24 to 30 per cent. albumen—air-dried meadow hay 7 per cent. One hundred bushels of sprouts,=1200 lbs., are therefore, as feed, equal to

$$\frac{1200 \times 27}{7} = 4,628 \text{ lbs. of hay,}$$

according to which the total quantity of sprouts used as fodder amounts annually to 28,925,000 lbs. of hay.

Those 25,000,000 bushels of malt yield at least 29,000,000 bushels of " grains," having a weight of 1,260,000,000 lbs. The amount of albumen contained in grains varies from 4 to 5 per cent., and, taking $4\frac{1}{2}$ per cent. as an average, 100 lbs. of grains are in their value as feed equal to 64 lbs. of hay, so that the total amount of grains used annually for feed is equivalent to 806,400,000 lbs. of hay.

The quotations of the above amounts of feed have no reference to the amounts of fibrine and starch, and as these substances greatly increase the feed value, an estimation of the approximate value of the wet grains as feed-matter at 1,000,000,000 lbs. of hay cannot be regarded as excessive.

The yearly consumption of hops in the United States amounts to 20,000,000 lbs., which, after having served their purpose in the brewery, furnish an excellent manure, especially for potato fields.

STATISTICS.

By A. Schwarz, Editor of the *American Brewer*.

I.—The Production of Beer in different European States.

The following statistical figures, compiled from official sources, will serve to show the noted increase in the production of beer in all beer-manufacturing countries; also the fact that the number of breweries has decreased, while the capacity of the remaining ones has actually increased.

1. North Germany.

There were in working order:

1868,	- - -	10,790 breweries.		1873,	- - -	10,172 breweries.
1872,	- - -	10,311 "				

They consumed:

1868,	- - - - - - - - - -	3,279,000 hundred weights of malt.
1870,	- - - - - - - - - -	3,765,000 " "
1871,	- - - - - - - - - -	4,230,000 " "
1872,	- - - - - - - - - -	4,860,000 " "
1873,	- - - - - - - - - -	5,835,000 " "
1874,	- - - - - - - - - -	6,225,000 " "

Whereof they produced:

1870,	- - -	771,956,731 litres.		1872,	- - -	972,190,299 litres.
1871,	- - -	881,136,455 "				

2. Bavaria.

Actually carried on:

1868,	- - -	5,091 breweries.		1871,	- - -	5,177 breweries.
1869,	- - -	5,105 "		1875,	- - -	5,125 "
1870,	- - -	5,131 "				

Wherein were produced in:

1868,	7,579,272 hectolitres of beer.		1872,	10,901,659 hectrs. of beer.
1869,	8,102,799 " "		1873,	11,351,920 " "
1870,	7,571,032 " "		1874,	12,074,740 " "
1871,	8,631,798 " "		1875,	12,600,153 "

3. Wurtemberg.

There were in 1871, 2,510 breweries in working order, which produced:

1871,	2,133,123 hectolitres beer.		1872,	2,801,085 hectolitres beer.

4. Baden.

Manufactured in:

1864,	446,833 hectolitres.		1870,	735,129 hectolitres.
1869,	676,907 "		1871,	814,893 "

5. Austria-Hungary.

In this country there were engaged in the manufacture of beer:

1868,	- 2,872 breweries.		1871,	2,694 breweries.
1869,	- 2,830 "		1872,	- 2,636 "
1870,	- 2,743 "			

Which together produced:

1868,	13,833,844 eimers.		1871,	18,015,732 eimers.
1869,	15,024,818 "		1872,	20,305,952 "
1870,	16,626,445 "			

(Lower Austrian measure, 2.34 eimers=one barrel.)

Vienna participated in above productions as follows, viz.:

1870,	3,677,222 eimers.		1873,	4,863,609 eimers.
1871,	4,025,307 "		1874,	4,386,855 "
1872,	4,337,453 "		1875,	4,378,991 "

According to the foregoing statistics, *Vienna alone produced in one year (1874), 1,874,800 barrels of beer, which is equal to the productions of the States of Pennsylvania, Illinois, Maryland, Louisiana, Montana, and Tennessee combined.*

The brewery of A. Dreher, in Klein-Schwechàt, produced during last year (1875), as much beer as the combined States of Michigan, Minnesota and Vermont.

6. HOLLAND

Manufactured:

1869,	1,143,000	hectolitres.	1872,	1,485,600	hectolitres.
1870,	1,198,040	"	1873,	1,528,000	"
1871,	1,270,800	"			

7. BELGIUM

Produced:

1870,	3,511,005	hectolitres.	1871,	3,462,183	hectolitres.

8. NORWAY AND SWEDEN.

Norway had 34 breweries, in which 250,000 hectolitres of beer were manufactured. In Sweden there have been, in 1870, 253 breweries, which produced the aggregate amount of 523,400 hectolitres of beer.

9. FRANCE.

The production of beer in France has not been in proportion with that of other countries, and as Alsace-Lorraine took a prominent part in the brewing of lager-beer, which production is included in the statistical reports of the German Empire, the present production of beer in France will probably not exceed 9,000,000 hectolitres for 1875.

10. RUSSIA.

It is a cause for congratulation to perceive the remarkable progress of the brewing trade in Russia, in spite of the large consumption of strong alcoholic beverages considered as belonging to the urgent necessities of life in that country.

There are already in existence large brewing establishments, managed by practical German brewers. From the incorrect and unreliable official reports it may be seen that the production of beer in Russia, in 1874, is not likely to exceed 1,160,000 hectolitres.

11. GREAT BRITAIN AND IRELAND.

In the United Kingdom of Great Britain the tax is paid on malt, therefore the official returns relate to malt produced and consumed.

The average estimate of malt to produce a barrel of beer is 2¼ bushels, but considerable quantities of sugar are used in the manufacture of beer also liable to taxation, as may be seen from the following statement.

Malt taxed for domestic use in bushels :

1870.	1871.	1872.	1873.	1874.	1875.
51,380,322	49,049,126	55,569,092	57,267,463	56,800,689	56,424,979

Sugar in hundred weights :

270,873	271,483	336,367	589,357	828,403	884,241

II.—PRODUCTION AND CONSUMPTION OF BEER.

The table below shows the proportion of the production of beer per head of population of beer-manufacturing countries, taking the production and consumption of the year 1872 as a reliable base :

Country.	Population.	Beer produced.	Equal per head.
Bavaria, - -	4,198,355	204,600,762 gall.	48½ gall.
Wurtemberg, -	1,818,484	62,246,348	34⅝
Belgium, - -	4,829,320	155,555,555	32⅖
Gt. Britain & Irel'nd,	30,838,210	792,946,467	26⅔
Saxony, - -	2,556,244	34,339,542	13½
Baden, - -	1,461,428	9,300,133	12⅖
Prussia, - -	24,693,066	216,042,288	8¾
Austria-Hungary, -	35,644,858	271,377,767	7⅗
France, - -	36,103,000	155,555,555	4⅖
Russia, - -	63,658,000	28,220,000	⁷⁄₁₆
U. States of America,	38,650,000	176,013,438	6⅗

The above figures do not represent the quantities of beer imported or exported from said countries, and if these are taken in consideration, Bavaria and Great Britain, both of which countries ship very remarkable quantities to other parts of the world, would considerably decrease their consumption per head, while Russia, France, and the United States, which all import beer, would show a greater consumption per capita.

The very slight consumption of beer in France and Russia is strange to perceive.

Owing to the immense quantities of wine grown in France, and the very low prices for which they are sold, the French prefer wine to beer.

It must not be inferred from the above table that in Russia the whole population participates in the consumption of its beer production; for it is a well-known fact that hardly one-tenth of the inhabitants drink beer, while nine-tenths indulge in distilled liquors of the worst sorts.

The consumption of beer in the United States, arguing from production and population, is almost equal to that of Prussia and Austria; it is to be considered, however, that the inhabitants of the latter countries must be regarded as regular beer-consumers, for beer, with them, is deemed a necessity of life,—while with us laws and municipal regulations exist for its suppression. It may be safely assumed, that only one-third of our people are consumers of malt liquors, and approximate calculation would therefore make our per capita rate three times as high as that of either Prussia or Austria.

III.—TAXATION OF BEER.

Beer, as a nourishing and refreshing beverage, deserves to be classed with meat and bread, as regards the subsistence and enjoyment of the masses.

It would conduce to the interest of the people, and would therefore be desirable and recommendable, to abolish all taxation, or at least levy a very slight one, upon its production and manufacture, but our financial policy seems to be not to understand the importance of this view.

The revenues annually obtained from beer in all the beer-producing countries form a valuable percentage of the aggregate taxation. The following table consists of an approximately correct compilement of taxes levied on a barrel of beer in different countries, viz.:

Great Britain and Ireland,	- $1.30	Baden,	- - - -	- $0.90
Austria, - - - -	- 1.20	France,	- - - -	- 0.70
United States of America,-	- 1.00	North Germany,	- -	- 0.50
Bavaria, - - - -	- 0.95			

The United States of America belong to the most heavily assessed of the beer-producing countries of the world.

Taking the official reports of the various countries of the world for the year 1872 as a reliable base, we find that the incomes obtained from beer taxation differ in their total amounts as follows:

Great Britain and Ireland,	- Sov. 72,229,000	6,978,371	9.74
Prussia, - - - -	- Th. 172,918,937	3,234,166	1.87
Bavaria, - - - -	- Fl. 87,144,606	9,617,126	11.03
Wurtemberg, - - -	- " 22,430,472	2,917,035	13.00
Baden, - - - -	- " 10,171,411	990,391	9.74
Austria, - - - -	- " 317,195,040	24,257,694	8.28
United States of America, -	- $ 359,101,231	7,800,000	2.17

www.ingramcontent.com/pod-product-compliance
Lightning Source LLC
Chambersburg PA
CBHW021446090426
42739CB00009B/1667